ARRANGEMENTS

ARRANGEMENTS

Peter Hughes & Eléna Rivera

AQUIFER

Published in the United Kingdom in 2022 by
Aquifer Books,
www.glasfrynproject.org.uk

ISBN: 978-1-8383587-5-4

Copyright © Peter Hughes and Eléna Rivera 2022

The right of Peter Hughes and Eléna Rivera to be identified as the authors of this work has been asserted by them in accordance with the Copyrights, Designs and Patents Act of 1988.
All rights reserved.

Cover Design: Steve Xerri

Contents

Arrangements 1

November (PH)	11
November (ER)	12
December (PH)	13
December (ER)	14
January (PH)	15
January (ER)	16
February (PH)	17
February (ER)	18
March (PH)	20
Mars (ER)	21
April (PH)	22
April (ER)	23
May (PH)	24
May Nights (ER)	25
June (PH)	26
June (ER)	27
July (PH)	28
July (ER)	29
July (Version 2) (ER)	30
August (PH)	31
August (ER)	33
September (PH)	35
September (ER)	36
October (PH)	37
October (ER)	38

Arrangements 2

February 2021 *(After 'Lines' by Wilhelmina Barns-Graham)* (PH)	43
Time Texture Vibrancy Creamy (ER)	44
March 2021 *(After Joan Mitchell's 'Sunflowers')* (PH)	46
Sunflowers – *After Joan Mitchell* (ER)	47
April 2021 *(After 'May' by Julia Ball)* (PH)	51
Spring Sailcloth - *After Julia Ball* (ER)	52
May 2021 *(After Sonja Sekula's 'The Voyage')* (PH)	53
May Sun - *(After Sonja Sekula's 'The Voyage' 1956)* (ER)	54
June 2021 *(After 'Orakel', by Li-Wen Kuo)* (PH)	55
June 2021 *(After Li-Wen Kuo's 'Orakel': Version 1)* (ER)	56
June 2021 *(After Li-Wen Kuo's 'Orakel': Version 2)* (ER)	58
July 2021 *(After Sheila Hicks)* (PH)	60
Two Directions at the Same Time - *After Sheila Hicks* 1 (ER)	62
August 2021 *(After 'Lost Voices', by Mary LLoyd Jones)* (PH)	64
What is There - *(After 'Lost Language' by Mary Lloyd Jones)* (ER)	65
September 2021 *(After Gabrielle L'Hirondelle Hill)* (PH)	67
Is Other And No One - *(After Gabrielle L'Hirondelle Hill, Spell #7)* (ER)	68
October 2021 *(After Maggie Hambling)* (PH)	69
When Levels Rise - *(After Maggi Hambling's The Corn Hall)* (ER)	70
November 2021 *(After 'Le jardin de la Fontaine à Nimes' by Danièle Ansermet)* (PH)	72
This Landscape Too - *(After 'Le jardin de la Fontaine à Nimes' by Danièle Ansermet)* (ER)	74
December 2021 *(After 'Southern Exposure' by Helen Frankenthaler)* (PH)	76
Antiphon - *(After Helen Frankenthaler's 'Southern Exposure')* (ER)	77
January 2022 *(After an untitled work by Etel Adnan)* (PH)	78
If I had four colors how would I place them into you? - *(After Etel Adnan's 'Untitled,' 2012)* (ER)	80

Arrangements consists of two sequences written between Peter Hughes and Eléna Rivera. Sequence one, 'Seasons', was written between November 2019 and October 2020. The poems respond to each other, but also to the solo piano suite *Les Saisons* by Tchaikovsky.

The second sequence, written between February 2021 and January 2022, responds to works by twelve women artists.

Some of these poems first appeared in Golden Handcuffs Review, Volt #23 and Tentacular. Also, 'September', by Eléna Rivera, was published as a limited edition broadside in collaboration with Oswaldo Garcia, for the N.Y Center for the Book Arts.

Eléna Rivera wishes to thank Cole Swensen, Anthony Hayward and MacDowell for providing space and solitude during part of the time when some of these poems were written.

Arrangements 1

November

        turning into strangers in the flat above
    the clocks go back
      along the rutted tracks

      through forests
      of the unimagined
        chestnut music

         chrysanthemum dusk
      at only twenty five to
          home made pumpkin soup

        offerings to convalescent skies
        an overpowering smell of more flags
         burning in the plaza

(PH)

November

can't turn back the clocks

    pattern of the profligate

flags in cold November

    air music's light offering vanished

breathless

now legs, arms, body stiffen

    in unseasonably chilly efforts

unimagined previously a pose rutted in repetition

    bluing the familiar restoration: "move"

shade of coral days

and trees the autumnal flower

    seen now beyond windowpanes

translucent and shy now what sense wasn't squandered

    the immigrant's prison-bars at dusk

a handful of how to's

(ER)

December

                heavy skies are roosting
          in the holly & the oak
                  the tallest & least visible

        loads are suddenly lit up
     exactly now
       acidic & yet crystalline
          refractions of the light

      through water turning
    in & out of us & ice
         with metamorphoses of memory
zoom out from its little cage fighters
to non-figurative drips & flickers

              into pathways trodden
           by these strange arrivals
            carrying the echoes

        of a party in the distance
     becoming fainter
        as they carry us away

(PH)

December

A death is announced (as in a mystery)
Prickly winds, flowers for a girl killed—
rapid transformation of form (from on high)

Approaching Winter Equinox, a date
doubling as light-post in all that cold rain
Let's make a list, clear the day drinking

Left the world with no memory (just mystery)
Nature is going/has gone to sleep (a bit of *noir*
inside and out) "The Affair Of" the whodunit

Small words brush in what the man called
the "narrow language" at a talk on poetry
and translation, a bit of tin being siblings

"A lie to stop pain" threads the mind
Twilight comes early, doesn't sit as easily
in the body a place of termination or free-fall

(ER)

January

    the earth's stuffed crust
        is scorched
     & from the top
of the revolving restaurant
   we're granted glimpses
      of incinerated
    foreigners & forest
heaps of tangible marsupials
the softly blackened outlines
      now dismembered
   by the winds that fanned
         by failure
          roar throughout the night

(PH)

January

a moment in the middle of the last
will I redress after a season of shifts
the remaining day in tomorrow's snow
forget the plan the thought of books
the pages when in winter the snow's
heavy on evergreens ink on a page
accumulates thoughts of elsewhere
link the forest to seared absent selves
freed briefly of my sonant habitation
write to Tchaikovsky's *The Seasons*
and hope I can see look in front of me
not frolic in the future lurking that trial
that binds to the earth even more debris
that grows breeds in the cold white sky
the space between shadow and light I
see from this window a photograph there
in my mind on this cold day the portrait
of "it is"—is it real or the island voice
that counts time tries to find what light
is where it's for sale where it comes from
how in the end details surface in a city
wracked with speed and future forward
lead here where time stops for a moment
in the midst of the last lifting of space
and the enduring project: "how we see it"

(ER)

February

here's another unelected twilight
granular as in an old Italian volume
    roosting in the clock with one hand shadowed

  by the other
wing is crudely carved
    as if by orphans

  emulating other people's parents making
simple spoons with grandma's hatchet
    & an elbow of storm birch

  the transformed green wood drying on the porch
where it has now turned dark
    we know the feeling

(PH)

February

Back again from snow covered arched alleys of pine and birch
    to jack hammers breaking pavement whipping up a rough kind of time—

knots we hold in our stomach just because we desired, so chin up
    that sweet turn has transformed into a rod to punish inside outside.

See me now the frog just about to jump into the pond! Look!
    Have I made a splash? Splash! Splash! Plop! Here's the flash

in the pan I set up, tied me up, then scrambled in different directions.
    I say no in my mind and yes with my tired vocal chords—Poor Tom

waiting at South Station about to embark on a new novel eating cold bacon.
    The Palestinian actress and a restless spirit pacing back and forth, poor heart,

train pulling out of the station, did we get the right ticket? Printing them
    out because we couldn't quite trust our cellphones which we clutched at.

We became close for a day sharing the ride with time and impatience
    on our way to where those who have made the numbers compose comfort.

The last experience disappears with the sound of the steel and rubber,
    countryside passing, more buildings appearing, a return to chopped up

time and the next appointment where a woman will prod this time
    and we'll wonder together if it was all worth it this measuring of the flesh.

I'll wear my yellow vest and let you guess to the kind I am referring to,
    I'm a-cold and you my ticket will lead me to "night and day beginning again."

(ER)

March

    a longer evening light begins to play
across the damp catchments of the valley
    & these eyelash fractals of resistance

the king is in his armoured counting house
    & has proclaimed that fire should be allowed
free reign to ransack woods & villages

    so as to reinforce the commonwealth's
immunity to future conflagration
    the slightly longer evening light plays on

around our temporary clearing
    a hint of fresh petal on the blackthorn
& a pair of long-tailed tits are building

(PH)

Mars

How to write of the present
    Daylight savings time thrust forward
new light—this season now "pandemic"

Stillness descends, city crocus
    bloom daffodils between empty
towers, some still work, having to—

having to move forward this month
    ruled by Ares in the Western Canon—
social distancing dilates, isolates

"And it's only been one week" he said
    laughing—third month, year 2020
stymied as gods extend the days

Self-isolation and soon in lockdown
    as the number of cases in N.Y. rise—
the propulsion of that rhythm forward

The population acclimates to crisis
    City birds chirp, trees burgeon,
high tech trills and sirens fill the air
                                    sirens   sirens

(ER)

April

so everybody's backing up
& burying their cheeses

some nights it's harder
to decide

die behind a skip

    or dance in front of thousands
to Tchaikovsky

(PH)

April

Did I mention
Did I mention pace
A generation hesitating
To fill the blue with attention

Hit the pot hard enough
They'll all see you, even on TV
There's that desire for lilacs
To scream, and dance

A few sleep til two
And find the slumber
Of melancholia leaning in
Like an empty street
Gardens blocked off

Still waiting for a shepherd
Who chose the music
The keys are in what chord
Did I mention procreation

Cry now that you can't stray
With a heart empty of future
Fish it out from the well
The tree and trauma still
For now, did I mention …

(ER)

May

      the instrument
    communicates
across the years of light
  the years of darkness
      Hubble ultra deep field images
        ways the past remains
          remote & palpable
        implacable & hard
      to calculate
      these musics or
the modulus of rupture
    for the self
        the neighbours
          & the state

(PH)

May
    Nights

The quiet of a city in quarantine, brisk
winds, then a pause, then a slight breeze,
noticing the notes of memory on a piano
glide—taste the ginger in your mouth

Scribe now of direct experience not
now a moment of consolation near
starlight—don't let me leave this place,
the white nights of this swaying season

Trees certainly can be playful in the dark
sway in the movement of the evening
inflorescence gone with the rain though
the water keeps the merry dripping high

A rolling residence in liquid introspection
A gazelle's gift as thoughts fly over trees
this season, with or without seasoning
the greening of lambent skies at dusk

as we precipitate toward our patterns
pondering our passage, slowing down
movement from a rapid romantic rise to
wave as you traverse an entire experience

    (ER)

June

Giovanni Bellini reflections
ripple through the surfaces of
autumn in an empty wooden frame

duck through a hole in the wall
& follow the course of the stream
uphill as far as the lake

watermarks through consciousness
eradicated olive trees
eradicated settlement

La Madonna dell'Orto
open now
closes 5.30

(PH)

June

    not so much "becoming" the instrument
            impervious to time I write a list of protests
                      until I forget something resonant in the heat

    a piano boating song washes over sirens
            the combat just as fierce inside as outside
                      a witness at home marking time like Crusoe

    curfew on the imagination—the theme masked
            something about the sequence, transmission
                      breathing in one theatrical image after another

    a carpenter bee nests in the wood chair
            Rapunzel in her tower writes notes to still
                      the noise, the curtain rises while unpacking

(ER)

July

I thought I heard Hart Crane murmur
    in the mind's sound
    through wires that modulated
    to the ghost of a mazurka
    in a lost line of Jack Spicer
or the insides of a broken radio
    in an empty Welsh hotel room
    where the song of someone else's
    lost companion & the ashes of
    forgotten gods sift downwards
through the twisted frames of pines & limes
    & carbonised imagined architecture
    to paraphrase the thinking
    which is rumblestrip glistening
    opposite plus waves & cats nearly
noiselessly steering through one fence
    then another across these
    moonlit gaps in cloud
    over hills to the east the stars
    are haunting three uninhabited planets
boots on gravel & the death of freedom

(PH)

July

The history of calamity or
the fragrant amber of the squash flower

Notes can be heard in the holes
"I hear the notes" trickle

Who drew the map?
Who made the border we are tethered by?

The gun, the fireworks, in season
What will you grill with that?

Most of the birds fled, but I'm here
parched in the summer sun

Ghosts in high rise forests
incrust towering echoes

(ER)

July (Version 2)

Fragrant amber summer sun

                surface anticipation

                in season

                tethered by

                calamity

"I hear the notes" we are

                in this country

                invisible ghosts

                towering echoes

                The border made

high-rise history

                Fireworks incrust

                and most birds flee

                but I'm here

                framed

(ER)

August

storms have rinsed
the trees the virus is
discouraging some tourists
in the middle
of the woods
there is no middle
of the woods
just an underlying
conversation joining
all these species
like a tawny owl
sat slowly owling
thoughts of tree
in tree slowly
grow over half
a dozen centuries
more seconds pass &
I remember
I must remember bread
while early evening
is creating bark rubbings
of consequent sounds
in floaters & this
translucent halo
posterior

vitreous detachment
an unmanned track
goes on ascending
to the first or last
of the Carneddau
descending to the river

(PH)

August

time doesn't stop
August sings
    a quick melody

a moment's translation
that anticipates sights of
    the rose-breasted grosbeak

where mind gets lost
in the tangle gives permission
    for the moment to echo

fast forward an Evening
Primrose opens only at twilight
    lost in a yellow description

the overflow of pine birch
maple that moment where
    what is near is so brief

resistance to the word
that captures Green Mountains
    mirrored in the flat lake

can't describe the harvest
the virus keeps families away
    gestures culled by the mind

crickets announce fall
twists and turns of perception
    future an approach fast forward

back to city narratives like
"Who lives, who dies"
    without benefit of allegory—

(ER)

September

we followed Elen of the Ways
into September with the hunt
rampaging in our heads
the line of fire advancing
through the forest
we thought about what happens
to the rain
the spore & languages
the individual notes
migratory & tidal
exceptional & accidental
phonemes lodged in feathers
the vowel in down
the stranded scraps
accumulate & nest
around the drowned

(PH)

September

       Saw the land
                    ignite
One thing, then another
                        Who saw the wind?

Fire   Flood   Virus
                      At the crossroad
                                    And we're all stuck in our boxes

      Beaten by our constant need / Even if it all falls apart

Dis-moi, je suis là
                "Who has seen the wind?"
What's next?
What's the rush?
                            to look for meaning, bitter-

     sweet "folds of feeling"
                      Land nowhere
                                  pass by

          Who counts the numbers

                            Clouds pass in a blue sky

(ER)

October

what about   I don't know   maybe
Slow Motion Blackbird by Chris Hughes
to go along with the Tchaikovsky
as the rain is softly falling
in the radio & over all these mountains
woods & buildings people's lives uneasily
co-existing with the branded news receptors
another acorn knocks on this thin cabin roof
the autumn oak leaves wonder when to fall
but this is when I make a brand new start
I'm calling it *The Modulus of Rupture*
a book of poems that might not see the light of day
but it's good to have a project
that doesn't fuck up an entire country
or world if you include the run up
well it's true that a lot of dreams these days
feel pretty tame compared to modern film
or politics & news of yet another death
Les says they used to make the coffins out of elm
as it was more hospitable to bugs & fungi
& so settled into other modes of life
sooner than some of us expected
this wet day began again with an exemplary blackbird's song
& this is just a temporary break

(PH)

October

What about
dawn drops
turn day
into a volatile
companion
a thrush
shakes
in the rain
rubbed, swept up
the art of
looking forward to
form
rustling leaves
crackle, raucous
in the wind, rain
a helicopter roams
in Harlem skies
Sigh
history in miniature
hidden
from ourselves
shaped
by four walls
the wee body
is lost
lopped

connections

ephemeral

the curves chromatic

darkness approaches

Ghosts hide

bumping against

limits

a turbulent evening

already

October

over here

producing

tempests

inside

the mind

must study

ourselves

at night

a child

remains

in the exchange

what did happen

to being

with others

a family of raccoons

give relief

in Riverside

Park

an attraction
where humans
melt
the majesty
of being
in place
yellow golden
aesthetic leaves
fall
an autumn night

(ER)

Arrangements 2

February 2021

(After 'Lines' by Wilhelmina Barns Graham)

the room is cold outside & lines
undecided waves of sound entrained
a murmuration of the air
the smudges are extinctions & unnamings
where our hands have rested
the room's that time I trimmed the dog
in autumn in the garden
not long before she died
& late next spring I notice all the birds
are lining their nests with her hair

(PH)

Time Texture Vibrancy Creamy

Stillness outside it is
snowing heavily white
out wind blows flakes
never knowing why I
look screen pictures

Computers serve now
painting online desert
abstract colors painted
landscape spread seen
between border image

I hear plaintive voice
inside I wanted to be
there in the line to make
the painting, cross over
the page elevate color —

destiny closer to snow
memory landscape Not
painting image screen
looked at online rather
pleasure unpredictable

In average moments
where color every day
life steps into a corner
to spread out a border
truth closer harbinger

Inspired by 'Line Series', 1983
Wilhelmina Barnes-Graham 1912-2004

(ER)

March 2021

(After Joan Mitchell's 'Sunflowers')

you can't reach from one side to the other
without moving your entire body
several steps along the dance of sap
& windswept paint to follow the sun
or hum an invocation to a changing
season inside & between us gravity
encouraging roots away from all this sky
& sunlight orchestrating a history of ideas
to do with turning our heads to the light
with a sense of energetic purpose such as
making tons of oily seeds for hamsters
or being as luminous as possible for
a few weeks on the way to more uncertainty
there's a gap down the middle to remind
us all about the plural step over it

(PH)

Sunflowers

After Joan Mitchell

Bold twins, step into this landscape

On canvas the two parts
deviate from rough, hairy peduncles

On the screen
seeing lines unravel
       in rosettes, simulated scenery

To be put alone in a vase
split at the center all body
upward then down—how the panels
were balanced, those bold lines
halved

      At the market
wrapped bunches of cut sun
      can fuse
          two of us—
     not the season yet
but in the picture

"plenty of wonder here"
unraveling

Intense red
    marks follow
        radiating,
catch the gaze, merge
    in turn, turn
        heads leaves
in a sequence
    70 or so species
        prominent
turn in a natural spiral
    bright corolla,
        bold lines, I drop
            my guard

A fibonacci sequence
    goes on forever
    I will stop with the final
brushstroke
    because otherwise, I
    might tell you
it's a good idea
    to continue beyond the synodic
    day of my green solitude

and blue ornamental
> garland
> that drapes the mess
of words reverberating
> untroubled
> inside the loose
swirls of eccentricity
> unravel
> terrifying beauty
so bold
> matched only
> by the mind

The sun
—swipe from top to bottom—
A bold line not fit
and then fits
> that's the surprise
>> even when cut off
>> from the original
>> intention of the panel
>> the pleasures reveal
>> pressures of the one
>>> flower making many
>>> as they pass through
>>> the blood basin of the body
>> shame pivots

crimson

on the rim of loneliness

    learning to appreciate

    what's long gone

poet of another season

the imaginary path

yields in time

    changes direction

    past the same meridian

        the golden number

        that requires a formula

            for how Helios

        hurries toward an equation

        to satisfy

        an expression

    A question that's there

    in the present arrangement

        combinations

        doubling identities

        infinite results

(ER)

April 2021

(After 'May', by Julia Ball)

we hold out pencils at arm's length & squint
while our minds paint something other
imagined through this valley in the sky
an ongoing invitation
to a further excursion
through the concluding seasons of a life
where imagined structures hover
in the breathing tones & shades of a Chardin
a rhythmic congregation
in a bog-standard communion
with softening light over & over the fen
an unintended relaxation of the throat
the water & goat willow I can see
after-images of old trajectories
a children's swing on an ash branch
in the bright garden of a house long gone
or the gap in the bushes that overlooked the bay
or the turn off at dusk onto the track
leading down to the cabin
or the headlights dipped to the road
twisting up to Frascati

(PH)

Spring Sailcloth

After Julia Ball

In March the spring scene cuts a crocus window
In April Aphros tempts tulips with endless space
Fragile constellations return golden to the page
Cluster of colors draw the eye to less inhibited
territory as it now funnels and filters downward
In May chromaticity between blue, yellow, violet,
siphoning the landscape into a single viewpoint
The advantage of a plant place, at different times
suffused with light, a private activity of being in it
in the realm where stillness takes over, opening
sensation of a particular moment in a landscape,
a landscape moving into the next green season
Here transition find the supports on the surface
I settle into my role as viewer reminded of the
present in the painting's being completely itself
made public and different at this time of year
where changes are pretty dramatic on canvas
& in the city sweet smell of crabapples & cherry

(ER)

May 2021

(After Sonja Sekula's 'The Voyage')

the rooms keeps changing colour
& turning into consciousness
  of multitudes
     spiral queues of close relations
choirs of gut bacteria
chanted notes that haven't faded
vibrant memories of journeys
  we thought had ended long ago
    a conference of garden peas
     swaying in spring netting
    nodes attached to rootlets
  under the tree at the bend in the road
a wordless song is murmuring
of populated patience
& what we said was
thank you for the terraces of flint
thanks for the cheese merchant's off-cuts
thank you for the beans that just keep coming
thank you for the disinfected gutter
  thanks for the hand-me-down cut-offs
  I wanted to be there in the line
   how thoroughly the world wears out its presences
    its nights & oceans
      feasts & prison camps
        its fingers interwoven in the rubble

(PH)

May Sun

(After Sonja Sekula's 'The Voyage' 1956)

Travel's majestic view lasts as long as an orchid

Under the sun memory thirsts for confluence
Only troubled by geometric roadmaps that
travel forward with an image stuck in my mind—
lines in another language forgotten by the studied
one, make holes send memories underground

Not able to look forward while I stood on the boat
that brought me to a brand new country—how could I
know it would erase my past, the one I once lived?
Perhaps lines touch? Thoughts cut up into pieces
of blues, purples, even orange—I scratched my way
making marks, a suitcase in hand, my heart full of lines
"then turned my back on it and walked away…"

A sun memory inconsolable intuits the irony of it all
The world and its weather patterns remembers conflux
everyday body becomes and members outside meet
A sign travels forward I shelved the rest in the wind

(ER)

June 2021

(After 'Orakel', by Li-Wen Kuo)

it is possible to stop

listening to the forest

you can see where Theodosius
had the sacred oak cut down

it spoke of a hole in the sky & a stoma
& it spoke of the African women
translating its whispers into songs of migrant birds

accompanied by shimmer & chime
bronze artefacts hung amongst its boughs
hold the shell logo up against your ear
& hear the muttered threats of death

says the gap

no need to rehearse how they
paint the eyelids of the 1% with murex
the mucous of a million sea snails

& dye the flags with Perkin's mauve
on undercoats of blood

it is possible to stop

listening to the forest

(PH)

June 2021

(After Li-Wen Kuo's 'Orakel': Version 1)

Ask the oracle where we come from,
and the gaping hole at the end, what of that?
A dark hole we think, stand before it open-mouthed

It gives rise to dark thoughts I think a foreign fear,
though it's in us, masked, measuring space inside,
enough, our own inexhaustible encounter with the end

Patience bears in itself the seed sound of language
High the task of letting oneself be multidimensional
The key into the logic of form and age, needs to ask

No breezy answers, heart beats wildly, wild the light
The possible grows at high pitch out of the center
The mirage and noise of the image is nothing

The cords invite us to slide right in, sing sparrows,
take us beyond the swatches of color, the bold
strokes into the jet-black gap, our own dark place

Dialogic the end, we left it blank too damn long,
made it enemy instead of following the paints length,
all the fading color, or treasuring the bold and large

that surround the cheap peach comfort that carries
such an encounter on a hot day in New York
Where does the gap come from? The hole there

in the pit of my soul? The large hole so feared, it too
is of the earth, our dear life asks the oracle to deliver
to answer the inexhaustible encounters with the end

(ER)

June 2021

(After Li-Wen Kuo's 'Orakel': Version 2)

—Dark thoughts, hear the heart beat
                Seed sounds of language
        No breezy answers

        The task of letting oneself be
multidimensional   Sing in the key of sparrow—
        the logic of the age, of age

        Heed the pull, up and down,
the gaping mouth where we're   invited to supper,
        that bears in itself the every day

        In the jet-black gap, our own dark place—
the large hole, so feared   it too is of the earth
        Ask the oracle, where we come from?

And the gaping hole at the end,   what of that?
Where does the gap come from?   the hole there
        Dear life ask the oracle to deliver, to answer

There are treasures left blank too damn long
        Made it an "enemy," the end,   instead of following
                the dialogic flow

Stand before the dark   open-mouthed,
surrounded by cheap peach comfort a hot day in New York,
and an inexhaustible encounter with the end

(ER)

July 2021
    (After Sheila Hicks)

reforesting the lining of the valley
    of the gut
the ghosts of suns
    suggested through the haze & ashcloth
as later light of day leans in
    on patched & shaded vespers
eye alight on shades
    of rust & tangerine
the yam & sandstone
    apricot & marmalade
the squash & amber
    clay & settling embers
honey & cinnamon
    marigold & whiskey
black pepper dust & blonde
    pecan & carob
caramel & copper
    heartwood of yew & wheat
coffee & bronze
    suede & chestnut
camel & Spanish grey
    precarious breath of dawn
holding graphite & cloud
    porpoise & slate

    iron filings & fossil
        lead & pebble
    small hours of late days
        some of the colours

(PH)

Two Directions At The Same Time

After Sheila Hicks,
For Keith DeCarlo

1.

I want to "do something to it" the woven textile "to do"
make it my own, see what there is and follow the play
of memory, its horizontal lifelines imbuing space threading
their varieties of vibrant colors, russet & brick for instance

The woof softens my saturated world of dark corners knots
absence & rules—autumnal colors of childhood, in Paris
at that embryonic stage when a child is still developing
feels textures close to her body, sees the many twists in
composition—on a bed that served as couch, dense textures
pillows, books, smoke, friends, children run between rooms

On the wall an artist's painting of an elegant horse, thin legs,
a thick torso and an upright head alongside an orange moon
Lines intertwine in that dark room filled with fibers of feeling,
shades of brown, and a sign in the WC that reads in English:
      "In the event of a nuclear attack, bend over, put your head
           between your legs, and kiss your ass goodbye"—

2.

Threads line the present
with material presence—
    I forgot to note the title of this present
    warp & weft, & because I forgot to note it
the poem is missing a guide in the present,
nothing to hang the poem on to besides a mood—

a child learns longing from a sign ties its shoes
learns about knots & confronts impatience—
    small protrusions encountered when trying
    to name parts & touch certain knots of sound

when the artist dies, he is removed from frame and family,
because leave-taking triggers more transience —
    all that remains is a large horse on the wall
    with a thick torso & thin legs in a ground-floor apartment
Language of amber unwinding, a beige, copper, umber poem

"le tissu tissé" a rectangle of woven fabric—
    "color is the mood determinant"
in an abstraction also silence & texture "inspire an expansive range
    of response"—in the present
    at a young age lines of color

(ER)

August 2021

(After 'Lost Voices', by Mary Lloyd Jones)

place value & an unacknowledged tally
etched high across the dome of the sky
or cave where a dark underworld sun still blazes
& trees & crystals merge imagining
a time & place beyond the damp & earthly
a book of hours tattooed & gouged in shale
old blood & river silt caked beneath the nails
constellations of familiar stepping stones
hovering alongside fish-scale stars & soot
branching zig-zags of an older language
an alphabet of trees envisioning
rickety bridges across the nocturnal
indigo echoes & charged white water
rushing to scour & rinse away the marks
we assumed were going to outlive us
Neolithic wi-fi password runes
knotted ropes from the *do-as-you're-told* box
lost songs from eradicated settlements
in flooded valleys & recollected seasons
so many water marks & firelit faces
fading into worn & shared abstraction
geometry drifting over ochre smudges
under an ecstasy of shooting stars
just out of shot bioluminescent
plankton delineate the shifting shores
of the first of our remaining nights

(PH)

What Is There

(After 'Lost Language, 2014' by Mary Lloyd Jones)

See the branch of the pine | Around language
        cultural inheritance, names, signs
The branch   'what is'   emphasizes
silence   —cup and ring marks on the wall of the mind
Spirals found   in the otherness   of utterance

Scarred landscape   speak   my body (mine?)
legacy of "mining"   What I could have felt as strength
a capacity for command   —the ultimate utterance—
turned into a tempest   (of ink, shapes)   division
Becoming vulnerable   is the landscape   of the unburied

Girl in a garden | In the midst of ruination/collapse
some say divide   and conquer   (what is the sense of that?)
Some shuffle words   draw lines   grow zinnias
touch walls | The bronze brick body
wants freedom   from constant   excavation

Observe   *nous voyons*   an obsidian impression
Name   the unrest   —charcoal marks
on the heart   —*mira*   *hay mucho*   wilderness
of signs   'violent men/and women of the cities'   the poet wrote
(NotashonestwithmyselfasIwouldliketobe)   now my mind is crowded

How do you know		"the place where you stand?"
How to yield to		that which disappeared
A trace	scratch	locked away
stray thought	poet	a line	spread out
disoriented	circles around	reads all

Who are we?	*It is time*	|	For the earth
a cave	labyrinth of possible outcomes
for all species on this surface	|	Swallow finds the right sticks
Why limit	or define	upon a central line
It is time	"to face ourselves	*dans n'importe quel langue"*

It was all there	in the marks	of our ancestors
in the territory	carried by bees	then forgotten
like early language	lost then	in the collision
of power	—reality fundamentally obscured	everything
I called out	was in me	—I couldn't see what was there

(ER)

September 2021

    (After Gabrielle L'Hirondelle Hill)

they gathered a diminished harvest   in pauses between storms

the living migrated into song   old recipes   embroidery

                        the spaces ache

the evidence of rape was inadmissible

Agnes Martin left the building   the building left the site
      foundation pits & trenches   silted up as sour rain scoured

            the final insubstantial notes from off the staves

oil seeped up   through slashes in the ground

tar hardened in gaps in the unspoken   extinctions & unnamings
little bumps barely registered   through plump new tyres

we still got drunk & dreamt   about each mineral   inhabitant organism
ever in this acre   joining hands & reaching out   from one side
of the encampment   to the other

(PH)

Is Other And No One

(After Gabrielle L'Hirondelle Hill - Spell #7)

Tobacco past in my lungs and in the painting . Wildness permeates
Precision was no line . "the veil that language builds around me"

Opened a beer can . Smoked a Cigarette . The romance of torture
Physical involvement projected onto paper . Flowers pressed into lines

Taste the coffee . Swirl it in your mouth . Ancient beak stance charms
Your sweet scent imbues the gallery . "What's controllable what's not"

Who tries to fit the letters into lines . I was saturated with tobacco
They say it takes seven years to change . Enjoyed my carelessness

Then it takes a while to recoup currency . When we forget the histories
I recognize now something about the surface . It's never empty

Never unbroken . What can I impart of my sensations . Tender trench
Don't close the gate on yellow . Consumers pass by without listening

The original tract . Exchange and trespass . A shoe cut from a magazine
Shred the turmoil . Not knowing why . How things got so desperate

All hang by a thread . Scribes ruled their paper by scratching on vellum
This took a long time . A childhood ruled by Jean Alexandre Séyès

(ER)

(Quotations from Daïchi Saïto)

October 2021

(After Maggie Hambling)

& then went down to the rafts
apocalypse now
across the media
disguised as spume
& mascarpone
your inner fish
still tempted by
the fantasy
of further evolution
owls & resubscription
stepping stones
the squeaky penguin
lost in the nasturtiums
now three fathoms deep
a caravan
sets out to sea
we clean the surfaces
& make a big risotto
in no more than
777 sentences
compare & contrast
hocus pocus by focus
with the hiss of shingle sewage
& convention speeches
earn a wet certificate
you may incorporate
inflatables & yodelling

(PH)

When Levels Rise

(After Maggi Hambling's 'The Corn Hall')

"here there is disaster, and possibility"

Saw it in a dream once, the uprising, tidal wave, tsunami
Salt water waves its evidence, "I was being pulled in"

Each day, each is different, each millisecond
—the moment the ocean breaks, the moment of arrival

Waves whooshing back and forth, crash, groundswell,
displacement, "Death will come, the sea will come"

"Sea levels rising" Meaning? "Sea levels rising"
—combine to conceive such mountains, valleys, crests

In the last 100 years, the sea level has risen by 6 to 8 inches.
What if: "I identify with the land that is being eroded"

Moods, the passing of time brings what type of tidings
Paint brush moves in the paint, represents a crash, a swell

Layering, load and lightness in a curve without thoughts
constant movement of emotion, will it overwhelm,

ease one in, swimming and at the same moment
the writer being pulled under the waves by rocks

as cormorants, seagulls and terns fly over the shore,
a city's harbor, and her own departure, seeking refuge

Where are the sounds when looking at a painting? I hear waves,
moments of excitement, of being brought to the deep end—

that "rapacious look" as Moore described it, different degrees of
tumultuousness—one adds sound because one imagines it

A memory of being caught in it, gripped by the force of it—
sea crashes onto sand—whose to say she came out of it alive, intact

If the South Pole ice melts, the sea will rise by 200 feet!
—saw it in a dream once or was that childhood, another country

The way waves break at the shore, the way a brushstroke moves
a goddess out of the foam, the curve of her body, tail twisting

Narratives lost at sea—in the colors—her mother a girl refugee
No end to it just rise and fall, the expanse of it—after departure

Family on a ship, traverses the great mystery that is the ocean
When is it time for the end, for the blues to come—this is it

> *Phrases with quotation marks are from an interview with Maggi Hambling.*

(ER)

November 2021

(After 'Le jardin de la Fontaine à Nimes' by Danièle Ansermet)

when my dad died
there was about four fingers
of emulsion left in the tin
he'd used to paint
the bedroom walls
so my mum put in
a cup of water just
to touch up the scuffs
when you enter the room
& by the light switch & curtains
now a decade later she's
still watering what's left
to make it go a little further
because she's 90
& you haven't been able to
find that shade for years
    & here are some of the camp sites
& meadows they cycled to after work
on Fridays & here is a clearing
in the New Forest that they made
their own & there's the Welsh slate fence
around a field they found one spring
together with two views of Ireland
bottom left is a picnic & a damp stain

from decades ago & through it all
you can just about make out
the shape of my dad's face
several popular poems
work along these lines
but paintings are different

(PH)

This Landscape Too

(After 'Le jardin de la Fontaine à Nimes' by Danièle Ansermet)

Do I get to enter the garden once again?
Eyes raised upward, unbroken sight-lines—
lift them so that you listen to what you see.
Green music appeases all the noise, lulls it—
the quieting down of the mind on a terrace
or sitting in the grass amidst the verdure.
In the foreground I glimpse a transparency,
fresh and filled with pine, oak, cypress.
Far down in the field the plants motionless
where the painter traces a path, a trail, lines.
She glimpses from behind, looks upward toward
emerald trees—an entrance where the walk
is just about to open into now, still in the past,
a kind of verdurous paradise in gradations,
remembered and experienced like the touch of
my mother's hand giving me a sense of safety.
As I walk along, alone in my thoughts, I note
the painting on the wall of my friend's house.
She picked it out, for the green of it, *knew*, and
bought it to enrich her place with its freshness;
its lime pine sage greenish-blue and yellow-green.
I can feel the leaves in my face touch memories

of a "remarkable garden," smelling a new rapport
with nature on the promenade, in the meadows,
on a hill, and if I climbed over the fence the child
would find, that I'm where you are, a favorite place.

(ER)

December 2021

(After 'Southern Exposure' by Helen Frankenthaler)

this morning Tchaikovsky feels comfortable
in just a suit & flip-flops
strolling through piazzas
then gazing through the currents of the Tiber
towards the absence of a future
& the desert of the unaccompanied

space walk in your head
 the sudden & eternal
space walk in your head
  disconnection
space walk in your head
   & end the year
space walk in your head
    the last song ever heard
space walk in your head
      click

it's beginning to look a lot like eczema

(PH)

Antiphon

(After Helen Frankenthaler's 'Southern Exposure')

To have an appetite	for everything
Between you and me	"Beauty is incendiary"
Does it need words?	The picture is a lie
I'm drawn to the top and bottom	lines
That's where there's movement	in such a bold field

"All at once"   How the colors interact   key
The screen's reproduction   emphasizes the light
Bright screen of the iPad   draws attention to the horizon
on the other side   the danger of too much   yellow
pale yellow   cream yellow   orange-yellow   orange-red   blood-red   red

Who can shut out light?   The image results from an effect of light
In landscape view   the presentation laid bare
One imagines   a meridional   southerly   burn
The scale is endless   chance affects everything
What do I expect of you?   There are no answers.

(ER)

January 2022

(After an untitled work by Etel Adnan)

she said the world was too tense
& that's why we need art

she said she'd done some tapestries
vulnerable to moths & tricky to mend

she said that now the greens are in this cotton box
the blues are in the biscuit tin

she said her favourite painters were photographers
of nature & poets who make nothing

from their work except you know magic
dispositions & sudden surges of ecstasy

she liked film & concertina books
she saw the mountain & she felt at home

distance no object four peaceful pigments
dry & side by side the colours travelled

far from their origins & also stayed
they should be given warmth & time to rise

alkaline emulsions you can rearrange
so that they stand up on their own

you see how much she disliked violence
& televised manipulations of the people

she said the world is too tense
& I came to painting through poetry

peaceful pigments come into the poem
the old dog limps in & goes to sleep

(PH)

If I had four colors how would I place them into you?
(After Etel Adnan's 'Untitled', 2012)

1.

There's so much I don't understand.

Doubt seeps into my appreciation

of blue. Hello a kind of peach that

becomes more pink, that mutates in

a desert or ocean. I want to name

the mountain, bring it back, trees

and rocks, will the summit to instruct.

Oh how to quiet the mind that fidgets

and suffers. I had a soup for lunch—

didn't notice at first the missing red.

　　"Naked woman lying down"

a moment drenched in abstraction.

2.

"The mountain became my best friend.
It was more than just a beautiful mountain;
it entered me, existentially, and filled my life."

3.

Woman laying down naked. I was in that desert,
even in the midst of winter, pummeled, and
startled by the light on the bough—touched by
an old tree, strutting—there were ways to see
a box of colors. Is that what it was? Colors
that go together which she then put together.

4.

float, inside the mountain I noticed

the little mountain, where I inserted

myself inside the tear—despair of

ever knowing anything at all

(ER)

                       Quotation by Etel Adnan